Tig the Cub

By Debbie Croft

Tig is a cub.

Tig is in his den.

Tig is not big.

But his mum is a big cat!

Tig has fun in the sun.

He can see a bug!

Mum got up.

Mum jogs to Tig.

Tig runs and runs!

Mum can see a big dog
at the den.

The big dog can see Tig!

Tig can not see the dog!

But Mum runs at the dog.

The dog runs off.

Mum and Tig go in the den.

Mum rubs Tig.

Rub, rub.

Tig hugs his mum.

Hug! Hug!

CHECKING FOR MEANING

1. Where is Tig at the start of the story? *(Literal)*

2. What was Tig doing out in the sun? *(Literal)*

3. Why does Mum run at the dog near the den? *(Inferential)*

EXTENDING VOCABULARY

den	What does the word *den* mean? If you took away the *d* and put the letter *h* there, what word would you make?
not	Look at the word *not* in the sentence, *Tig is not big*. What does this mean? Make a list of other words that are opposite in meaning, e.g. *up* – down; *in* – out.
jogs	Look at the word *jogs*. How many sounds are in this word? What is the sound at the end of the word? Find other words in the story that end with the same sound – *runs*, *rubs*, *hugs*. Explain that all these words tell readers about the actions in the story.

MOVING BEYOND THE TEXT

1. What other words do you know that are the names of animal homes, e.g. pen, stable, kennel?

2. How do animals keep their babies safe in the wild?

3. What could have happened if Mum stayed in the den instead of going outside?

4. Why do you think Mum and Tig rubbed and hugged each other?

SPEED SOUNDS

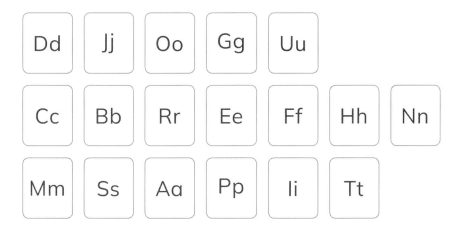

Dd	Jj	Oo	Gg	Uu

Cc	Bb	Rr	Ee	Ff	Hh	Nn

Mm	Ss	Aa	Pp	Ii	Tt

PRACTICE WORDS

Tig

cub

den

not

big

But

mum

jogs

Mum

fun

sun

up

hugs

got

rubs

rub

bug

runs

Rub

hug

dog

and